The Teton Sioux

The TETON SIOUX

People of the Plains

BY EVELYN WOLFSON

NATIVE AMERICANS
THE MILLBROOK PRESS
BROOKFIELD, CONNECTICUT

MY SINCEREST THANKS FOR
INFORMATION GATHERING, READING,
AND EDITING TO DOROTHY TWEER,
DACIA PESEK, AND WILLIAM WOLFSON.

SERIES CONSULTANT

Karen D. Harvey, Ed.D.
Assistant Dean, University College
University of Denver
Co-author, *Teaching About Native Americans*

Cover painting "Horse Owner's Society" by Kills Two,
reproduced from H.B. Alexander's *Sioux Indian Painting*
courtesy of Yale University Library

Photographs courtesy of:
North Wind Picture Archives: pp. 13, 14, 18, 33, 39,
45 (right); Art Resource/ National Museum of American
Art: p. 20; Museum of the American Indian: p. 23 (left);
South Dakota State Historical Society: pp. 23 (right),
25; Thomas Gilcrease Institute of American History and
Art: p. 27; American Museum of Natural History: pp. 30–
31; Amon Carter Museum, Fort Worth: pp. 36–37; Library
of Congress: pp. 42, 44–45, 46; The Bettmann Archive:
p. 48; Allen Russel/Profiles West: pp. 51, 52–53.

Library of Congress Cataloging-in-Publication Data
Wolfson, Evelyn.
The Teton Sioux : people of the plains / by Evelyn Wolfson.
p.   cm.
Includes bibliographical references and index.
Summary: Examines the history, folk culture, way of life,
and contemporary problems of the Teton Sioux Indians.
ISBN 1–56294–077–5
1. Teton Indians—History—Juvenile literature. 2. Teton
Indians—Social life and customs—Juvenile literature.
[1. Teton Indians. 2. Indians of North America.] I. Title.
E99.T34W49   1992
978'.004975—dc20   92–4633   CIP   AC

CONTENTS

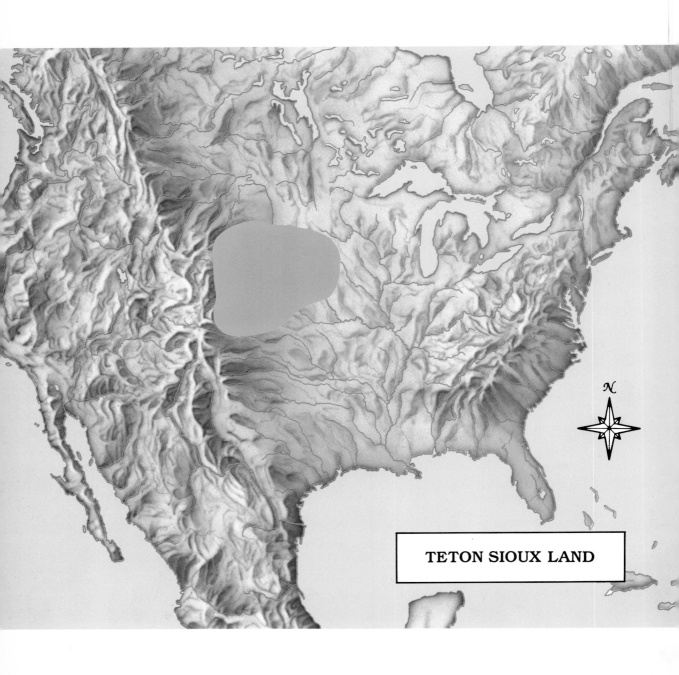

TETON SIOUX LAND

FACTS ABOUT
THE TETON SIOUX

GROUP NAME: Dakota ("friend")

DIVISION: Tetons (Lakota)

BANDS: *Oglalas*, Scatter One's Own
Brulés, Burnt Thighs
Miniconjous, Those Who Plant by the Stream
Two Kettles, Two Boilings
Hunkpapas, Those Who Camp at the Entrance
Sans Arcs, Without Bows
Sihasapas, Blackfeet

GEOGRAPHIC REGION: Northern plains
(northeastern Wyoming, western Nebraska,
and parts of North and South Dakota)

LANGUAGE: Siouan (Lakota dialect)

HOUSE TYPE: Tipis framed with three poles

MAIN FOODS: Bison meat, other game,
wild plants, and berries

TRANSPORTATION: Horses

Chapter One

BISON, HORSES, AND GUNS

The young Crazy Horse stood on a hill overlooking the North Platte River. Below, riders approached the camp of his people. Quickly, he rolled his bison blanket into a ball and threw it high into the air: once, then twice. The signal meant bison or enemy were coming.

Women left their partially scraped bison hides stretched over the ground. Children stopped swimming and took cover along the river. Men ran to their tipis to get weapons. Crazy Horse watched as Chief Conquering Bear and his braves gathered in the camp.

Before long, soldiers arrived. A nervous interpreter introduced Lieutenant John L. Grattan and thirty of his soldiers with a sweep of his leathery hand. They had come to arrest a young Miniconjou, High Forehead, for killing a cow. But High Forehead claimed the cow he killed had wandered into the village. Chief Conquering Bear reminded Grattan that the cow—and its white owners traveling west—had been crossing Teton Sioux territory illegally. Unaware that Conquering Bear and his braves were armed, Grattan opened fire. Conquering Bear and several of his men died. But when the fight was over, Grattan and his entire command had been killed.

The year was 1854, and the place was present-day Wyoming. It was the beginning of a long series of battles between the U.S. Army and the Tetons. Crazy Horse, witness to this first battle, was destined to become one of the greatest and most feared of the Sioux warriors fighting to take back their land.

IN THE BEGINNING ■ The Tetons had not always lived in the territory along the North Platte River. Long before Columbus came to America, the Teton, Yankton, Yanktonai, and Santee Sioux lived in the Ohio River valley. Eventually, they moved to the moist woodlands of southern Minnesota, where they lived in bark-covered wigwams. In winter they tramped over waist-deep snow on large, well-designed snowshoes. In summer they traveled along freshwater lakes and streams in birchbark canoes. In a region too cold to grow corn, wild rice was the staple food and kept the Sioux well fed all year.

The Sioux got their name from their Minnesota neighbors, the Chippewas, who spoke the Algonquian language. The Chippewas called them Nadewisue (nay-da-wee-soo), which means "treacherous snake." (The Sioux themselves preferred *Dakota*, a Siouan word that means "friend.") French trappers shortened Nadewisue to Sioux. The word survived as a name for the people and their language.

The Tetons separated from the Yankton, Yanktonai, and Santee Sioux in the mid-1600s. The Oglala, Brulé, Miniconjou, Hunkpapa, Sihasapa, Sans Arc, and Two Kettles groups made up the Teton nation. They spoke the *Lakota* language. The Tetons followed herds of bison, or American buffalo, south to the Missouri River valley and west onto the Great Plains. Within fifty years the Tetons had abandoned rice gathering for bison hunting.

The Tetons hunted bison on foot using lances and bows and arrows. They had to be clever, well organized, and patient to get enough meat for everyone. Bison traveled in herds, and when one of them was killed, the rest stampeded. So hunters learned to take as many animals as possible at one time. They did it by quietly surrounding herds on foot or by setting grass fires to drive them into corrals or off cliffs.

Large wolflike dogs with upturned tails served as pack animals for Teton families. They pulled small A-shaped frames, or *travois* (tra-voy). Travois were made by attaching two poles to the shoulders of a dog. The poles dragged on the ground, and a small platform held them together. Hunters did not travel long distances because dogs could not carry heavy supplies. Dogs also dragged travois over the grassland, chasing rabbits and other small animals.

HORSES CHANGE TETON LIFE ▪ In the mid-1700s, horses that escaped from Spanish ranches in Mexico came north. They were captured wild or traded from Native Americans who lived on the southern plains. The arrival of horses changed the lives of the Tetons more than any single event in their history. Unlike dogs, which lived on the same food as their masters, horses were content to graze on fresh green grass, as the bison did. They were obedient, worked hard, and required practically no care.

The Tetons had developed a *nomadic* way of life (moving from one location to another in search of food) that depended on bison long before they had horses. But horses moved them across the plains with greater ease. They kept pace with galloping herds of bison and made hunting easier. Horses pulled larger travois and carried family members who could not walk. They were such good pack animals that the Tetons often called them sacred dogs.

For the first time, the Tetons could ride out of the tall-grass prairie and close to snow-clad mountains that looked near enough to touch but were days away by horseback. Horses showed Teton families clear blue sky and land covered with herds of grazing bison. Having been surrounded by trees, shrubs, and tall grass, the Tetons were excited by the wide open views of the plains.

Teton men worked hard to round up wild horses. They tamed and trained them in sturdy wooden enclosures. When the horses tired of galloping and bucking, young braves slid thin rawhide straps into their mouths and rode them. Before long, men spent all their free time raising and training horses. They trained horses to gallop alongside racing herds of bison while they shot a steady stream of arrows.

Horses became so important to the Tetons that they often stole them. Horse stealing became a popular game among plains nations. Braves crept quietly into enemy camps and cut loose herds of horses. Sometimes they took valuable horses right from under their owners' eyes. Like today's fancy sports cars, the fastest and most beautiful horses disappeared first. Horses became a measure of wealth for the Tetons, although generally they frowned upon riches.

With the arrival of the horse, life changed forever for
the Teton Sioux. Because horses could carry heavy loads
and pull travois, as shown above, the Tetons were able
to move easily across the plains in search of bison.

At almost the same time that the Tetons discovered horses, they also discovered guns. Guns came from traders or enemy nations defeated by the Tetons. The deadliness of guns and the swiftness of horses combined to make the Tetons successful hunters and fearless warriors. U.S. General George Cook, an ex–Civil War officer, once said that the Tetons had the best cavalry on the plains. Their horses were so well trained that riders could hold the reins with one hand and use the other to shoot arrows, hurl lances, and reload rifles.

Fighting was an important part of plains tradition. Every nation had a most-feared enemy. The Tetons attempted to be the most feared of all nations living on the plains. They captured the homelands of the Omahas, Arikaras, Kiowas, and Cheyennes. By the early 1800s, they had claimed most of western Wyoming, Nebraska, and parts of North and South Dakota.

When the Tetons discovered the Black Hills of South Dakota, they believed the earth had finally opened its arms to them. The Black Hills were very much like their ancestral homeland and became sacred to them. Rightly named, the hills rose darkly above miles of soft green grassland. The Tetons believed that *Wakan Tanka*, the Great Spirit, had covered the northern plains with thick green grass to attract bison. Then he had given the Tetons horses. Bison and horses became a boundless source of power for the Tetons.

Finding water for the horses was not easy on dry prairie land. And controlling the wild animals until they were tamed and trained took patience, sensitivity, and strength.

Chapter Two

LIFE ON
THE PLAINS

By the late 1700s the Tetons had given up most of their woodland traditions. They had swapped snowshoes and canoes for horses. They had exchanged bark-covered wigwams for tipis. Bison meat had replaced rice.

Bison hunting was easier than rice gathering, but it made year-round nomads out of the Tetons. Everything they owned had to be portable, lightweight, and useful. Pottery was too heavy and fragile to carry, baskets too time consuming to make, and wood scarce. But these sacrifices were small when compared with the many things bison gave the Tetons: food, warm clothing, robes, blankets, hides to cover tipis, and bone and horn to make utensils and tools. Dried bison dung even served as fuel for the fire.

THE TIPI CIRCLE ▪ The Tetons lived in family groups called *tiyospes*. Every tiyospe had a leader, or sometimes many leaders of equal status. Leaders were men whose families were important and owned many horses. They took charge of moving, choosing campsites, and maintaining order. Leaders had to be good organizers, brave, honest, and fair. If they were not, they lost their position.

Before tiyospe leaders chose campsites, they sent scouts ahead to look for bison herds. Leaders tried to camp near a grazing area favored by bison. While women and children unloaded travois and set up tipis, men secured horses and helped spiritual leaders prepare for bison ceremonies.

In their ancestral homeland, hunters would build temporary shelters when they went hunting in winter. The shelters were cone-shaped and covered with bark. When the Tetons moved to the Great Plains, skin-covered tipis, like bark shelters, were small at first. But tipis had to shelter extended families—not just parents and children, but grandparents and other relatives, too. So they eventually became large and comfortable.

Men went to the mountains to get framing poles to build tipis. They chose tall, straight lodge-pole pine trees that were at least 20 feet (6 meters) high. After the trees were taken down, they were left in the sun to dry. Dry wood was lighter and easier to haul home.

Women made tipi frames by tying three of the lodge-pole pine trees together at the top. They hoisted the poles into the air and spread them out at the bottom. Then they rested eight or ten more poles against the frame to make it strong.

Teton women made tipi covers out of bison hides. First, the women drove stakes into the ground and stretched the stiff hides across them. They cleaned excess flesh and muscle from the hides using scrapers made from bone or elk antler. After the hides dried, they were cleaned again. This time women removed

It was the women's job to do the hard work of turning bison hides into robes and other useful items. Tools made from bones or antlers were used as scrapers to clean the hides in the first step of the tanning process.

the fur. Stiff, clean hides were soaked in water for several days. Then animal fat, brains, and livers were rubbed into them to make them soft. Afterward they were rinsed and rubbed back and forth over a twisted rawhide thong to dry them out. They were made waterproof by smoking over a slow fire. The whole process was called tanning.

Women kept count of the number of hides they tanned. After each hide was finished, they made a black dot on the handle of their scrapers. When ten hides had been completed, they made a red dot on the opposite side. After they had finished a hundred hides, they made a circle around the base of the handle.

When it was time to make a tipi cover, women asked friends to help. The average-size tipi required fifteen bison hides to cover it. Two dozen women took twelve days to sew together the hides to make a cover. When the cover was finished, it was spread out on the ground. Then it was tied to the top of a long pole. The pole was raised, and the cover was wrapped around the frame. Above the doorway two wing-shaped flaps marked the smoke hole. A row of wooden pins below the smoke hole held the cover together. Below the pins a separate hide wrapped over a U-shaped willow frame covered the doorway. The door faced east, the direction of the rising sun. Women often added strips of rawhide with porcupine quills, feathers, and horsetails above the door.

Tipis stayed cool in summer and warm in winter. In summer the bottom edges of the tipi were rolled up so that breezes could blow through. In winter the edges were weighted down with soil, snow, and rocks to keep out the wind. The cone shape of the tipis kept heat close to the ground where people sat. Dew cloths hung around the inside from shoulder height to the floor.

This sketch, by nineteenth-century artist George Catlin,
shows a Sioux encampment by the Missouri River.
Hides can be seen stretched between stakes on the
ground and hung from frames to dry in the sun.

They kept out moisture. They also created a pocket of air that acted like insulation. Men painted dew cloths with important battle scenes, dreams, and visions.

Tipi circles were the center of life, as homes and communities are today. Families ate, drank, and talked about the day's events around the fire. Young married couples built tipis close to their parents' tipis. One family often included a man, his wife and children, a grandparent, and unmarried aunts or uncles. Grandmothers were important family members because they helped women tan buffalo hides, preserve food, cook, gather wild foods, and take care of young children. Some grandmothers made salve for newborn babies from dried red clay mixed with bison fat.

Inside a tipi, men sat at the northern end and women at the southern end. The head of the family leaned on a woven willow backrest supported by a tripod. Others sat on furry bison-skin rugs. Several families living in one tipi created a sense of privacy by piling household items between them.

TETON VALUES ▪ Children learned to share and trust others when they were very young. Kindness and good behavior were rewarded with praise. Selfishness was frowned upon.

Children learned to respect elders and avoid closeness with members of the opposite sex. Brothers did not make eye contact with sisters, men with mothers-in-law, nor women with fathers-in-law. As in all families, children learned how to act by watching, listening, and imitating adults.

Families praised hunters and warriors and encouraged them to be proud of their accomplishments. They gave festive parties to honor heroic deeds. Women prepared special foods, and heroes were paid extra attention.

Fancy headdresses filled with many feathers showed off the wearer's importance. Feathers were symbols of honor, and men often risked their lives to earn them. They were awarded for saving another person's life, stealing horses, hand-to-hand combat, and *counting coup*, or touching the enemy.

Counting coup was an extreme test of courage for every warrior. It was a terrifying challenge that required getting close enough to make eye contact with an enemy, touching him with a bow, arrow, stick, or bare hands, and running. Counting coup was dangerous and exciting, much more difficult than shooting from a distance. Getting close enough to smell the enemy required true fearlessness.

Women were expected to be hardworking and faithful. They gained admiration for their endurance, strength, and patience. Families boasted about women's skills with the same enthusiasm they had for men's. Besides making tipis, women were also dressmakers and tailors. They made soft deer- and elkskin breechcloths, shirts, and leggings with fringes for men and boys. For themselves and their daughters they made silky-smooth buckskin dresses beaded at the yokes and shoulders.

Women spent many hours creating beautiful beadwork designs on animal hides. Competition among the women was strong. Before European traders brought glass beads, women decorated hides with the thin, hollow quills that cover porcupines. Porcupine quills had to be pulled from dead animals and sorted by size. They were dyed many colors but were not as bright as glass beads. Glass beads needed no preparation and came in brilliant colors. The beadwork of Teton women was highly valued

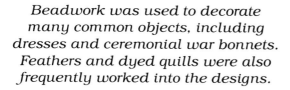

Beadwork was used to decorate many common objects, including dresses and ceremonial war bonnets. Feathers and dyed quills were also frequently worked into the designs.

by other Native Americans and by European traders. It was often traded for valuable horses or weapons, or for fine European clothing.

Married women were encouraged to bear many children. When she wanted a divorce, a woman placed her husband's clothing outside the family tipi. Men who wanted a divorce simply did not come home.

The Tetons took sweat baths in specially built lodges called *sweathouses*. These small, dome-shaped airtight lodges had an open space through which hot rocks were passed. Men sitting inside poured cold water over the rocks, and the little lodge filled with hot steam. The men inside then began to perspire. The Tetons believed that taking sweat baths cleansed their minds and bodies.

Throughout the year the Tetons thanked and honored the Great Spirit, Wankan Tanka, a mysterious force that they believed controlled everything in the universe. The Tetons believed that everything in the universe had a spirit. Humans, plants, wild animals, wind, rain, sun, water, and thunder were all related and dependent on one another. The Tetons believed that failing to hold important ceremonies and rituals or disobeying tribal laws made spirits angry. These angry spirits caused illness.

An herbalist, *shaman*, or dreamer had to be called upon to cure illness. The Tetons believed that these specialists had the power to control spirits and knew rituals to drive away angry ones. Shamans often prescribed special brews that caused vomiting, perspiration, or diarrhea and flushed illness out of the body.

*In this photograph from the early 1900s, a shaman sits
before a bison skull altar. Shamans played an important
part in the spiritual life of the Tetons, conducting ceremonies
to drive away angry spirits and cure illness.*

Chapter Three

THE SPIRIT OF THE LAND

The Tetons could tell by looking at the moon how many days remained before a new moon would appear. Roughly every twenty-eight days a new moon brought a change in the season. So they named the changing moons to describe seasonal changes. For example, April was called the Moon of the Birth of Calves, August the Moon of Ripe Plums, and December the Moon of Frost in the Tipi. Years were also given names. Sometimes these names told about an important event or happening in the world. Because of an eclipse, the year 1869 was remembered by some Tetons as the Year the Sun Died.

SPRING ■ April marked the beginning of each new year. In the spring families left winter camps and began annual rounds of food gathering and hunting. Women and children tapped box elder trees for sap and gathered fresh fruits and berries. Men hunted deer and elk, but not bison. They let bison graze so they would be fat in the fall.

Families spent a lot of time outdoors playing games. A favorite game played by young boys required that players wrap the ends of short sticks with balls of mud. Only the tips of the sticks

When the weather was mild, the Teton Sioux
enjoyed many forms of outdoor recreation, including
stick-and-ball games similar to lacrosse.

Shooting the Buffalo

Hoop-rolling games, such as Shooting the Buffalo, were popular with the Tetons and developed hunting skills.

Materials:
    60-inch (1.5-m) round hoop
    Permanent black ink to mark hoop
    36-inch (90-cm) sticks, one for each team member
    Paint to color team sticks

Mark a large hoop as follows:
    Three single lines (10 points)
    A small rectangle (20 points)
    A cross (10 points)
    Five straight lines (20 points)

The symbols should be spaced evenly around the hoop. They represent the directions of the compass—south, west, north, and east.

Players decide the highest number of points needed to win the game. The game starts when the hoop is rolled between two teams. A player on each team throws a stick at the hoop as it rolls past. When the hoop falls, the sticks lie against it. Points are awarded according to the mark nearest the stick.

showed. The object of the game was for each team to cover the opposing one with mud. After a starting signal, boys threw the mud at their opponents. The mud made a whooshing sound when it was flung through the air.

In spring, men went on *vision quests* to seek personal guardian spirits. They took trips into the mountains, where they spent four days in an isolated place. During their stay they did not eat or drink. Fasting and solitude often brought on visions. Spirits appeared in these visions disguised as wolves, deer, elk, or other animals. If a wolf appeared to a man, it was believed that wolves would protect and guide him for life. To be sure that guardian spirits stayed with them all the time, young men often carried arrows in quivers, or holders, made from the skin of the animal.

The Tetons created special societies for men who had acquired guardian spirits. The Akicita Society was open to young men sixteen years or older. Akicita members were responsible for maintaining order during bison hunts and camp relocations. They also stopped fights and punished offenders. Each season a different member became leader. Families gained importance when several members belonged to the Akicita Society.

SUMMER ▪ The Tetons lived far apart, and summer *solstice* celebrations, when the sun's position in the sky marked the beginning of summer, brought everyone together. Runners traveled from one camp to another to announce the time and place for meeting. Bands of the Tetons met on the plains and arranged their tipis in circles. They reserved the center of the tipi circle for socializing and hosting public ceremonies, songs, and games. Tiyospe leaders traded information about enemy and herd movements. Couples courted, and families exchanged gossip. Men smoked the sacred pipe and wrapped their pledges in smoke to send to the Great Spirit.

The sacred Sun Dance ceremony was the most important part of the summer solstice celebration. Sun Dance ceremonies lasted twelve days. First the Tetons went into the mountains to find posts to build a Sun Dance lodge. They framed the lodge with twenty-eight posts. The posts represented the number of days that passed between new moons.

Next a perfectly straight pole was set up in the center of the lodge, with a bison skull for an altar. The pole represented the center of the earth. It reached toward the sky and connected the

This picture of the third day of the Sun Dance ceremony was painted by Shortbull, a chief of the Oglala Sioux, in 1902. Those who survived the last days of the ceremony became shamans.

sky to earth. Since bison symbolized all of life, a bison-skull altar was appropriate.

The last four days of the ceremony were spent dancing. Men danced and sang to honor bison, horses, bears, and Wakan Tanka. The most important dance of all was the Sun Dance. Formal dancing began when men circled the sacred pole, attached to it by long ropes tied to small wooden skewers that stuck through the flesh on their chests. During the first few days of dancing, men kept their feet on the ground. Then the ropes attached to the skewers were pulled up, and occasionally the men's feet left the ground. Eventually, men who planned to become shamans had their feet completely lifted off the ground.

They hung in the air until their flesh tore and they fell. This last dance was called Gaze at the Sun Suspended. No gift belonged more completely to a man than his own flesh. And it was the most personal gift he could offer to Wakan Tanka. Men who remained conscious and survived the rigors of the last day became powerful shamans. They wore their chest scars with honor.

FALL ▪ August, the Moon of the Ripe Plums, marked the end of summer and the beginning of the most important hunting season of the year. Families gathered for communal, or group, hunts. Sometimes herds were close enough for families to camp nearby while men hunted. Other times men chased the herds, and the families stayed behind. If the families had to move to winter campsites before the hunters returned, they left behind a marker to show the direction in which they traveled. The marker was a long pole stuck into the ground. Attached to it was the shoulder bone of a bison. On the bone the leaders drew the outline of a travois, hoof prints, and the family's symbol.

Boys started to hunt soon after they learned to ride. Often they joined organized hunts after they had killed a bison calf. On these hunts every hunter had a specific job. To learn how hunts were conducted, young men often served as water boys and fire keepers.

After a hunt, women went to the site to retrieve the animals. Organs and other pieces of meat that spoiled quickly were eaten immediately. But most of the animal was packed on travois and taken home.

Women sliced bison meat into thin strips and hung them to dry. They set small, smoky fires underneath the drying racks to

Before the introduction of guns, Native Americans on the southern plains used bows and arrows to hunt bison.

keep flies away. Women made *pemmican*, pounded dry meat mixed with fat, berries, and peppermint leaves. Men took it on hunting trips because it did not spoil. Today we call pemmican beef jerky.

Families shared bison meat, bones, organs, horns, and hides. Men made knives, scrapers, and needles from bones. They made cups and bowls from horns, and they made bags and containers from organs. Hooves yielded glue, and tendons were made into string. Hides were made into tipi covers, blankets, robes, and moccasins. Untanned hides, called rawhides, were used to make cooking pots, ceremonial drums, and war shields.

■ 33 ■

WINTER ■ In October, the Moon of the Fallen Leaves, snow began to fall and families settled in winter campsites. The Tetons often took refuge in the Black Hills with herds of wintering bison. Or they arranged tipis by streams or under overhanging cliffs near bison wintering grounds.

In the warmth of the tipis children played around the fire while their parents worked. Men repaired tools and utensils. Women sewed, decorated clothing, and made dolls. Fathers and grandfathers helped young boys make bows and arrows.

In winter the Tetons enjoyed playing games outdoors. Throwing It In was a top-spinning game played on the ice. Players twirled tops toward a row of five evenly spaced holes cut in the ice. Spinners tried to get their tops into the center hole. Like skilled pool players, boys could often name the hole they planned to land their tops in before spinning.

Storytelling was a popular form of indoor entertainment during winter evenings. The Tetons often told stories about their origin. Some stories described the adventures of important spirit figures such as Iktomi, who was both a hero and trickster. Iktomi's adventures told the secrets of wild animals. For example, one story revealed where to find animal tracks and how to know deer tracks from elk tracks.

Sometimes the storytellers used symbols drawn on dew cloths to remind them of exciting war stories and to jog their memories about important dreams. After a long evening of storytelling, the children were then asked the following night to repeat all the stories. It was a challenging memory test that everyone enjoyed. The Tetons developed keen memories by listening to and repeating stories.

Chapter Four

SOLDIERS AND STRANGERS

Before the Revolutionary War, land west of the Mississippi River was considered wilderness. After the war, it became Indian Territory. Eastern Native American nations whose land had been taken by settlers were sent to live there. Teton territory was left untouched, however, until beaver became scarce in the East and trappers needed to find a new source. So in the early 1800s, trappers opened a post along the North Platte River in the heart of the Teton territory.

Soon beaver became scarce in the Teton territory, too, and the trappers left. In 1849 they turned their post over to the U.S. Army, which named it Fort Laramie. Soldiers came to the fort to protect pioneers who traveled the nearby Oregon Trail. The Oregon Trail was an old Indian trail that went from near present-day Kansas City, Missouri, to Oregon. Pioneers used the trail for almost ten years. They traveled in wagon trains loaded with women, children, and supplies. They headed west encouraged by land deals and the promise of a new life.

But as the wagons rattled across the grasslands, they scared away bison, killed the grass, and left deep wheel ruts in the soil. Because bison began to avoid their favorite grazing

In this painting by Charles M. Russell, a wagon train determined to cross the southern plains is attacked by Native Americans equally determined to protect their hunting grounds.

grounds, Teton hunting habits were forced to change. The Tetons robbed and harassed the wagon trains in an effort to drive the trespassers away. Eventually, a peace treaty, the 1851 Treaty of Fort Laramie, was signed. It allowed pioneers to use the Oregon Trail and promised the Tetons $50,000 a year for fifty years for the land.

THE SIOUX WARS BEGIN ■ For three years after the Treaty of Fort Laramie was signed, relations between the Tetons and settlers were relatively peaceful. But in 1854 a cow left the trail and was killed by a Sioux brave, and United States soldiers under Lieutenant John L. Grattan attacked Conquering Bear's camp on the North Platte River.

For the next ten years fighting broke out from time to time. In 1862, pioneer leader John Bozeman decided to take a direct route across Teton territory between the gold fields of Montana and the East. He forged a new trail, the Bozeman Trail, in defiance of the treaty. The Teton chief Red Cloud and others met at Fort Laramie to plead for the enforcement of the treaty. They discovered that the army had made plans to build a string of forts along the Bozeman Trail. Red Cloud believed that the army's actions were a declaration of war. He vowed to fight.

By 1866, new forts were under construction. Congress had ordered that the Bozeman Trail be widened, improved, and protected. Teton and other warriors rallied to support Red Cloud, who was keeping the new Fort Phil Kearney under siege.

Red Cloud and his braves attacked the fort and trail day and night. They were joined by Arapaho, Cheyenne, and Kiowa braves who had fought the U.S. Army on the southern plains. Red Cloud's forces grew to be the strongest in the West. They kept the Bozeman Trail closed for two years.

Red Cloud, shown here about 1890, was chief of the Oglala Sioux in the 1860s when the war for the Bozeman Trail was fought. Even though the Sioux won a victory when the army forts along the trail were abandoned and the trail was closed, Red Cloud and his people lost their traditional way of life.

The Fetterman Massacre

A veteran Civil War fighter named Captain William Fetterman came to help defend Fort Phil Kearney in 1866. His slogan was: "Give me eighty men and I will ride through the whole Sioux nation."

Fetterman volunteered to search for some men who had left the fort to cut logs and had not returned. The young Sioux warrior Crazy Horse, who had witnessed the killing of Chief Conquering Bear and Lieutenant Grattan at the North Platte River years before, waited for Fetterman and his eighty men. Also waiting to ambush them were a Cheyenne named Big Nose and 1,500 warriors. Big Nose shook his head back and forth, bared his broad white teeth, and taunted Fetterman just beyond the reach of his bullets.

Fetterman took the bait and waved his men forward. When they were firmly trapped below a ridge, hundreds of warriors rose and opened fire. In what became known as the Fetterman Massacre, Fetterman and his entire command were wiped out. Eighty-one men—one more man than Fetterman had said he needed to wipe out the Sioux nation—died below Long Ridge Trail.

Eventually, the Bozeman Trail became too expensive to maintain, and the army agreed to close it. Red Cloud was offered another treaty. After two long years of fighting, he and his braves had won a dramatic victory. But Red Cloud refused to sign the Fort Laramie Treaty of 1868 until the army abandoned the forts.

It was thrilling for Red Cloud and his men to see the forts' flags come down and hundreds of soldiers march away. They immediately burned the forts to the ground and thanked Wakan Tanka for the return of their beloved land.

For a number of years, Red Cloud and his people tried to re-create their old ways. But life on the plains was changing rapidly. The introduction of trains did more harm than the settlers or soldiers ever did. The railroad carried thousands of reckless hunters who shot bison from the train windows. Buffalo guns (heavy guns with wide-diameter barrels) could hit and kill a bison from a mile away.

LITTLE BIGHORN ▪ By the 1870s, bison had begun to disappear from the Great Plains, and the Teton way of life disappeared with them. Before long the Tetons could not find a bison skull to make a Sun Dance altar. Instead of using fresh hides, the Teton women had to patch and repair the old, tattered skins that covered their tipis. When they ran out of hides, the women used canvas taken from wagon trains. And people began to starve.

With great sadness, Red Cloud agreed to take his people to live on a reservation. Fortunately, it included their sacred Black Hills. But the Tetons had not been on the reservation long when gold was discovered, after U.S. Lieutenant Colonel George A. Custer and his soldiers came to the Black Hills in 1874.

The effect of the railroad on southwestern Native Americans was devastating. Whole herds of bison were wiped out by each trainload of hunters who plowed into their midst and shot wildly.

When the news got out, miners came by the thousands. Embarrassed that Teton land protected by treaty was being illegally invaded, the U.S. Army at first tried to protect the Black Hills. But miners ignored warnings to stay away. The same army that had won the Civil War ten years earlier declared that it was unable to keep out the miners.

Red Cloud met with U.S. officials, who first offered to buy the Black Hills from the Tetons. Then they offered to buy just the mining rights. But Red Cloud would not agree to sell the land.

Meanwhile, Crazy Horse and a powerful Hunkpapa Sioux medicine man named Sitting Bull left the reservation. More food was needed to feed their people, so they went to the grasslands to hunt. They and their followers met others on the plains who had left their reservations in search of bison. Native Americans throughout the region were starving because they did not get the food promised to them by the U.S. government. So they gathered on the banks of the Little Bighorn River to plan an escape route to Canada.

On June 25, 1876, Custer and the 7th Cavalry attacked the encampment on the Little Bighorn River. However, Custer underestimated the number of warriors camped by the river. The Sioux warriors wiped out Custer and more than two hundred soldiers in the Battle of Little Bighorn.

FINAL DEFEAT ▪ After their victory at what became known as Custer's Last Stand, the Sioux suffered a series of defeats at the hands of the U.S. Army. Sitting Bull and his followers fled to Canada. But Crazy Horse stayed in the United States where he was promised reservation land for his people. After rumors spread that he planned an uprising, Crazy Horse was arrested in September 1877. Confronted by armed soldiers, he panicked and tried to escape. A nervous young soldier stuck a knife in his side, and Crazy Horse fell to his knees, seriously wounded. He died several months later.

Sitting Bull returned to the United States from Canada in 1881 and was sent to live at Standing Rock Reservation in present-day South Dakota. For a time, Sitting Bull traveled with Buffalo Bill Cody's Wild West show, but eventually he returned to the reservation. He joined the Catholic Church, which had been established on the reservation, and turned his home into an orphanage.

On June 25, 1876, Custer (in the center in this roman-ticized view) and more than 200 of his men paid for their attack on the Sioux at Little Bighorn with their lives. Sitting Bull, (above) a leader of the Sioux attack at Little Bighorn, was known to his people as a statesman and spiritual leader.

About this time, something happened that renewed the hopes of many Native Americans, including the Tetons. A new religion, called the *Ghost Dance* religion, was started by a young Paiute named Wovoka. Wovoka had a vision in which dead relatives and ancestors of Native Americans came to life. He saw lakes and streams turn blue again, the air become sweet and fresh, and thousands of bison return to the land. In his vision, a dance would make this dream come true.

This scene of the Ghost Dance was published in a newspaper of the time. The Ghost Dance so terrified U.S. officials that they ordered the ceremonies stopped. When the Sioux refused, many were arrested, and Sitting Bull was killed.

The Ghost Dance was simple but required dedication and endurance. Participants had to dance for three days and nights without food or water. It became known as the Ghost Dance because dancers entered a trance and saw the ghosts of their dead relatives.

U.S. government officials were frightened by the large number of Native Americans who gathered for the Ghost Dance. They feared the gatherings would cause riots. So they banned the dancing. When the bans were ignored, officials ordered the arrest of several respected Native American leaders. Sitting Bull was first. He resisted arrest and was killed. His friend, Big Foot, a Miniconjou leader, worried that he would be next. So Big Foot escaped with 106 braves and 234 women and children.

It was December 1890, the Moon of Frost in the Tipi, when Big Foot and his followers left the reservation. They headed across the moon-like landscape of the badlands. Big Foot had pneumonia, and his people were cold and hungry. They could not travel fast. When the troops finally caught up with them, Big Foot was ordered to set up camp at Wounded Knee Creek.

U.S. Colonel George A. Forsyth took command of the Wounded Knee encampment. He ordered Big Foot and his warriors to turn in their weapons. When only a few weapons were brought forth, Forsyth sent soldiers to search the tipis. Frightened women and children screamed as soldiers turned their homes upside down. Suddenly their screams were interrupted by the sound of a shot. It echoed down the creek and over the hills. The rifle of a deaf Native American, who was wrestling to keep his weapon, had discharged.

Instantly, soldiers fired on the unarmed people. Then the cannons went off. Some soldiers died. But before the attack was over, Big Foot and more than two hundred men, women, and children had been killed or wounded. Native Americans remember the tragedy as the Massacre at Wounded Knee.

The massacre at Wounded Knee in 1890 left hundreds of Sioux dead and signaled a final defeat for Native Americans.

Chapter Five

THE SIOUX TODAY

Few Ghost Dances were celebrated after the Massacre at Wounded Knee. The Sioux and other Native Americans had been defeated once and for all. They were forced to adapt to reservation life, where food remained scarce and they lived in poorly constructed wooden houses rather than in tipis. A life of counting coup, hunting bison, and stealing horses was no longer possible.

Today about half of all Sioux live on reservations in the United States and Canada. Nearly sixty thousand live on eight reservations in South Dakota. There are also two reservations in North Dakota, four in Minnesota, and one in Nebraska. Five bands of the Sioux live in Manitoba, Saskatchewan, and Alberta, Canada. Some Sioux own farms and ranches or live in cities.

Over the years, some Sioux have become activists—those who fight for the rights of their people. Some joined the American Indian Movement (AIM), a group founded in 1968 that stages demonstrations and other public events to gain support for Native American causes. Unfortunately, sometimes these events become violent. In 1973, at the Pine Ridge Reservation in South Dakota, where the Wounded Knee Massacre took place, activists began to argue with tribal elders and U.S. officials over old treaty

In some respects, life on a reservation today is like life in any American community. But government-supplied housing and education are often very poor, and jobs are difficult to find.

agreements. The arguments turned into shoot-outs. Activists put up wooden barriers and exchanged gunfire with soldiers for two months. One member of AIM and two others were killed. Two years later, two members of the Federal Bureau of Investigation (FBI) died in a clash at the same site.

In 1980, the U.S. Supreme Court ordered the government to pay $105 million to a group of Sioux tribes for land taken illegally. But the Sioux refused the money and called instead for the return of part of the Black Hills.

Although life on a Sioux reservation can be hard, many Sioux have become well educated and successful. They have attended schools on and off the reservations. They have distinguished themselves as doctors, lawyers, teachers, scholars, writers, artists, and philosophers. Many Sioux who leave the reservations for education and training return to help improve living conditions there. Unemployment on the reservations is often over fifty percent.

One of the greatest challenges that the Sioux have faced successfully is that of combining their sacred traditions and

In December 1990, on the 100th anniversary of the Wounded Knee Massacre, scores of Native Americans participated in the Big Foot Memorial Ride across the plains of South Dakota.

customs with modern ways. Many who have converted to Christianity, for example, continue to practice traditional beliefs. Horses are no longer used for hunting or for war, but the Tetons are skilled in rodeo competitions. Many speak the Siouan language, conduct traditional ceremonies and rituals, and practice age-old arts and crafts. Men offer the sacred pipe to Wakan Tanka and send messages in the smoke of their fires. They keep alive the practices of sweat baths, vision quests, and the Sun Dance. They remember and honor their heroes—Crazy Horse, Sitting Bull, and Red Cloud.

A TETON STORY:
WHITE BUFFALO WOMAN

The Sioux believe that the owner of a white buffalo hide holds vast supernatural power because white buffalo, or albinos, are sacred beings. This story tells why.

Long before the Sioux had horses, they hunted on foot. But sometimes bison herds did not come, and people got hungry. Once, when bison had not come for many months, two young scouts went out on the plains to try calling them.

Before long, a small speck appeared on the horizon. The scouts jumped with joy. The speck came closer: It was a beautiful young woman with flowing black hair. She wore a white buckskin robe decorated in colors the scouts had never seen before. She carried a bunch of sage and a pouch.

One scout reached out to touch the woman. Immediately he was struck by lightning, and his body turned into a pile of ashes. The other scout, who stayed a respectful distance from the woman, stared in awe. He did not doubt that she was sacred.

Then the woman said to the frightened scout, "Go tell your people to build a sacred medicine lodge, and I will come."

The scout ran back to his village as fast as possible with the news. Men began to build a lodge. When it was complete, white buffalo woman came. She carried the bunch of sage and the pouch. She told the people to put an altar made from red clay and a bison skull in the center of the lodge.

When the medicine lodge was ready, buffalo woman opened the pouch and took out a handsome pipe. She held the stem with her right hand and the bowl with her left. The bowl was filled with fresh, sweet-smelling tobacco. Then she took a chip of buffalo dung from the fire and lit the pipe. She told the people that they had been chosen to keep it. It was a sacred pipe.

Buffalo woman walked in a circle around the lodge to symbolize the circle of life. She said the pipe bowl was made of stone to represent the buffalo and the flesh and blood of men. She said the stem symbolized all that grew on the earth. She lifted the pipe east, west, north, and south and then toward the sky and down to the earth. She said that the smoke that rose was the breath of the great Grandfather Mystery.

Then buffalo woman offered words of advice and guidance. She told the women that their work kept people alive and was as important as that of warriors. She told them that they were mother earth. She explained to men and women that the making of a pipe bound them together. Men carved the pipe and women decorated it. She reminded children that they were precious because they would be the next generation to smoke the sacred pipe.

When she was finished, buffalo woman got up and left the lodge. She had not gone far when she stopped and rolled over four times. After the first roll she became a black buffalo; the second time a brown one; the third time a red one. On the last roll she became a beautiful white buffalo calf.

Soon after she disappeared, herds of buffalo came. Men went hunting, and families thanked buffalo woman for feeding them. After that, buffalo gave themselves willingly to the people. They gave meat, warm clothing, tipi covers, tools, and utensils— everything the Sioux needed for their life on the northern plains.

IMPORTANT DATES

MID-1600s	The Teton Sioux migrate to the Great Plains
MID-1700s	The horse comes to the Tetons
1851	Red Cloud signs the Treaty of Fort Laramie
1854	John L. Grattan and U.S. soldiers wiped out by Tetons at North Platte River; Sioux Wars begin
1865	Construction of Fort Phil Kearney begins
1866	The Fetterman Massacre
1868	Red Cloud signs second Treaty of Fort Laramie
1871	Red Cloud and his people move to a reservation
1874	Custer's expedition discovers gold in the Black Hills
1876	Custer defeated at the Battle of Little Bighorn
1890	Ghost Dance religion started by Wovoka; Massacre at Wounded Knee
1968	American Indian Movement founded
1973	Fighting at Wounded Knee on Pine Ridge Reservation
1980	U.S. Supreme Court orders federal government to pay eight Sioux tribes for land taken illegally
1990	The Sioux observe the 100th anniversary of the Massacre at Wounded Knee

GLOSSARY

counting coup. Touching an enemy to prove one's bravery.

Dakota. A word in the Siouan language that means friend. Also the dialect spoken by the Santee division of the Dakota people.

Ghost Dance. A Native American religion that swept across the Great Plains in the late 1800s.

Lakota. A dialect of the Siouan language spoken by the Tetons.

nomadic. Moving constantly from one location to another for food.

pemmican. Finely pounded dried meat mixed with fat and flavored with berries and mint leaves.

shaman. A man with special supernatural powers and the ability to remember and interpret dreams and visions.

solstice. The time of year when the sun is farthest from the equator. The summer solstice (about June 22) marks the beginning of summer, and the winter solstice (about December 22) marks the start of winter.

sweathouse. A small wigwam-like structure. Inside, cold water is poured over hot rocks to create steam. Sweathouses are used for ritual purification.

tiyospe. A group of families who belonged to a common Teton band.

travois. An A-shaped frame made by attaching two poles to a dog's or horse's shoulders and used to carry supplies.

vision quest. A period of solitary fasting designed to bring on visions.

Wakan Tanka. A mysterious force known as the Great Spirit that travels through and controls everything in the universe. According to Sioux tradition, it exists in every one of nature's beings.

BIBLIOGRAPHY

*Books for children

Andrist, Ralph K. *The Long Death.* New York: Macmillan Co., 1964.

Bear, Luther Standing. *Land of the Spotted Eagle.* Lincoln, Nebr.: University of Nebraska Press, 1978.

Culin, Stewart. *Games of the North American Indians.* New York: Dover Publications, 1975.

Curtis, Edward S. *The Sioux and the Apsaroke,* from Vols. 3 and 4 of *The North American Indian,* ed. Stuart Zoll. New York: Harper & Row Publishers, 1975.

DeMallie, Raymond J., and Douglas R. Parks, eds. *Sioux Indian Religion.* Norman, Okla.: University of Oklahoma Press, 1987.

Dorsey, J. Owen. "Games of Teton Dakota Children." *American Anthropologist* (October 1981): 329–46.

Eastman, Charles A., and Elaine Goodale Eastman. *Wigwam Evenings.* Lincoln, Nebr.: University of Nebraska Press, 1990.

Erdoes, Richard. *The Sun Dance People.* New York: Random House, 1972.

Erdoes, Richard, and Alfonso Ortiz, eds. *American Indian Myths and Legends.* New York: Pantheon Books, 1984.

Ewers, John C. *Teton Dakota.* Berkeley, Calif.: National Park Service, 1938.

*Franklin, Paula A. *Indians of North America.* New York: David McKay Co., 1979.

*Freedman, Russell. *Buffalo Hunt.* New York: Holiday House, 1988.

*_____. *Indian Chiefs.* New York: Holiday House, 1987.

*Goble, Paul. *Buffalo Woman.* Scarsdale, N.Y.: Bradbury Press, 1984.

*_____. *Gift of the Sacred Dog.* New York: Macmillan Co., 1984.

Grinnell, George Bird. *When Buffalo Run.* Norman, Okla.: University of Oklahoma Press, 1966.

Grobsmith, Elizabeth S. *Lakota of the Rosebud.* New York: Holt, Rinehart and Winston, 1981.

Hamilton, Charles. *Cry of the Thunderbird.* Norman, Okla.: University of Oklahoma Press, 1972.

Hassrick, Royal B. *The Sioux.* Norman, Okla.: University of Oklahoma Press, 1964.

Hebard, Raymond Grace and E.A. Brininstool. *The Bozeman Trail.* Vol. I. Lincoln, Neb.: University of Nebraska Press, 1990.

Kopper, Philip, and the Editors of Smithsonian Books. *The Smithsonian Book of North American Indians.* Washington, D.C.: Smithsonian Books, 1986.

Leitch, Barbara. *A Concise Dictionary of Indian Tribes of North America.* Algonac, Mich.: Reference Publications, 1979.

Lowie, Robert H. *Indians of the Plains.* New York: Natural History Press, 1954.

Macfarlan, Allan, and Paulette Macfarlan. *Handbook of American Indian Games.* New York: Dover Publications, 1958.

McGinnis, Anthony. *Counting Coup and Cutting Horses.* Evergreen, Colo.: Cordillera Press, 1990.

McHugh, Tom. *The Time of the Buffalo.* Lincoln, Nebr.: University of Nebraska Press, 1972.

McLaughlin, Marie L. *Myths and Legends of the Sioux.* Lincoln, Nebr.: University of Nebraska Press, 1990.

Neihardt, John G. *Black Elk Speaks.* Lincoln, Nebr.: University of Nebraska Press, 1961.

_____. *Indian Tales and Others.* Lincoln, Nebr.: University of Nebraska Press, 1988.

Powers, Marla A. *Oglala Women.* Chicago: University of Chicago Press, 1986.

Powers, William K. *Yuwipi.* Lincoln, Nebr.: University of Nebraska Press, 1982.

*Rickman, David. *Plains Indian Coloring Book.* New York: Dover Publications, 1983.

*San Souci, Robert. *The Legend of Scarface.* New York: Doubleday, 1978.

*Sneve, Virginia Driving Hawk. *They Led a Nation.* Sioux Falls, S.D.: Brevet Press, 1975.

Terrell, John Upton. *Sioux Trail.* New York: McGraw Hill Book Company, 1974.

Tillett, Leslie, collected and ed. *Wind on the Buffalo Grass.* New York: DaCapo Press, 1976.

Utley, Robert M. *Indian, Soldier, and Settler.* St. Louis, Mo.: Jefferson National Expansion Historical Association, 1979.

Viola, Jerman J. *After Columbus.* Washington, D.C.: Smithsonian Books, 1990.

Webb, Walter Prescott. *The Great Plains.* New York: Gosset & Dunlap, 1931.

Wellman, Paul I. *Death on the Prairie.* New York: Macmillan Co., 1934.

Wissler, Clark. *Indians of the United States.* New York: Doubleday & Company, 1966.

*Wolfson, Evelyn. *Growing Up Indian.* New York: Walker and Co., 1986.

Wyman, Walker D. *The Wild Horse of the West.* Lincoln, Nebr.: University of Nebraska Press, 1963.

Zitkala-Sa. *Old Indian Legends.* Lincoln, Nebr.: University of Nebraska Press, 1985.

INDEX